Contents

MAP: where the main religions began

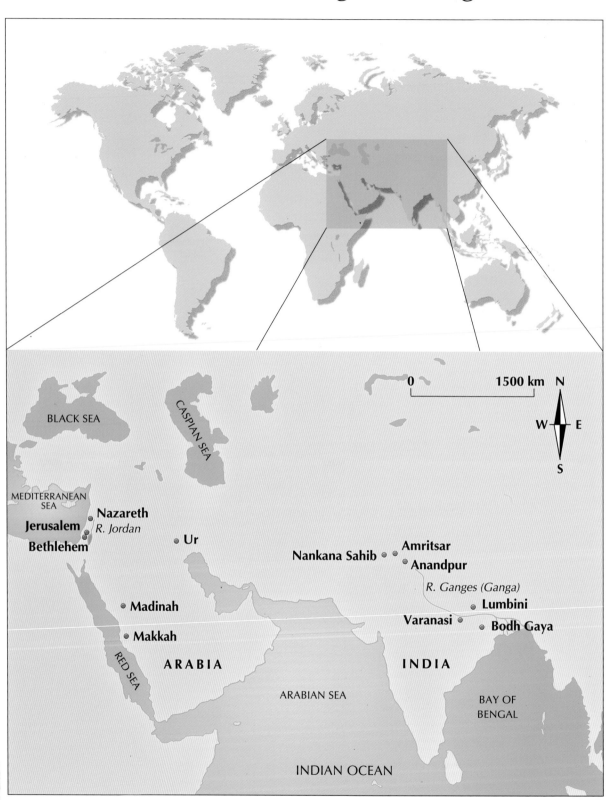

Discovering Religions

Islam

Sue Penney

Heinemann Educational Publishers,
Halley Court, Jordan Hill, Oxford OX2 8EJ
a division of Reed Educational & Professional Publishing Ltd

MELBOURNE AUCKLAND FLORENCE
PRAGUE MADRID ATHENS SINGAPORE
TOKYO SAO PAULO CHICAGO PORTSMOUTH (NH)
MEXICO IBADAN GABORONE JOHANNESBURG
KAMPALA NAIROBI

© Sue Penney 1987, 1995

First published 1987
Revised edition published 1995

99 98 97
10 9 8 7 6 5

British Library Cataloguing in Publication Data
A catalogue record for this book is available from the British Library

ISBN 0 435 30468 2

Designed and typeset by Visual Image
Produced by Mandarin Offset
Printed in Great Britain by Bath Press Colourbooks, Glasgow

Acknowledgements

Religious Studies consultant: W Owen Cole

Thanks are due to E H Bladon for reading and advising on the manuscript.

The publishers would like to thank the following for permission to use photographs:
The Ancient Art and Architecture Collection p. 32; Kayte Brimacombe/Network p. 16;
Circa Photo Library pp. 24 (below), 41; Sally and Richard Greenhill p. 7; Robert
Harding Picture Library pp. 26, 33, 34 (left); The Hutchison Library p. 39; Christine
Osborne Pictures p. 38; Peter Sanders pp. 8, 9, 10, 11, 12, 13, 15, 17, 18, 19, 20
(top), 23, 24 (top), 35, 36, 37, 40, 42, 43, 44, 45, 46, 47; Frank Spooner Pictures
p. 31; Zefa pp. 6, 20 (below), 22, 29, 34 (right).

The publishers would like to thank Zefa for permission to reproduce
the cover photograph.

The publishers have made every effort to trace the copyright holders. However, if any
material has been incorrectly acknowledged, we would be pleased to correct this at
the earliest opportunity.

TIMECHART: when the main religions began

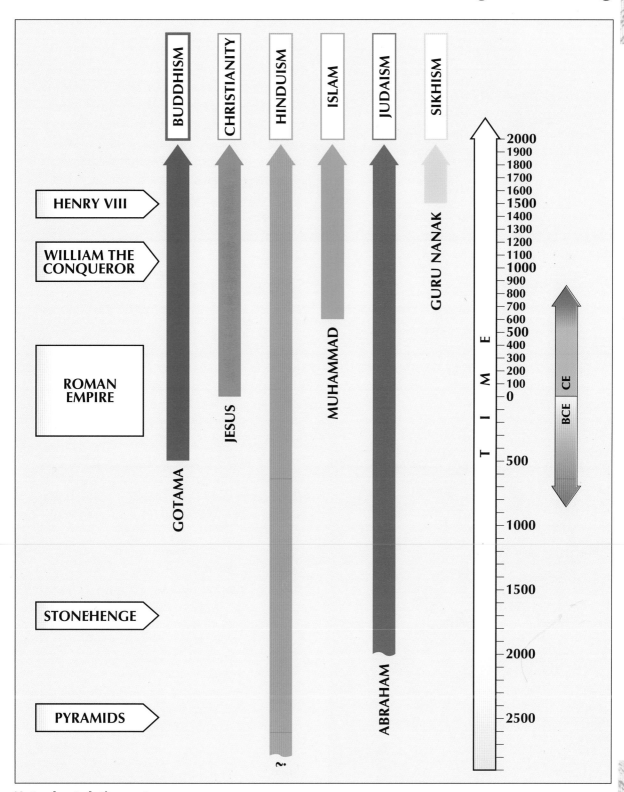

BUDDHISM

CHRISTIANITY

HINDUISM

ISLAM

JUDAISM

SIKHISM

HENRY VIII

WILLIAM THE CONQUEROR

ROMAN EMPIRE

GOTAMA

JESUS

MUHAMMAD

GURU NANAK

STONEHENGE

PYRAMIDS

ABRAHAM

T I M E

2000
1900
1800
1700
1600
1500
1400
1300
1200
1100
1000
900
800
700
600
500
400
300
200
100
0

500

1000

1500

2000

2500

CE
BCE

Note about dating systems

In this book dates are not called BC and AD which is the Christian dating system. The letters BCE and CE are used instead. BCE stands for 'Before the Common Era' and CE stands for 'Common Era'. BCE and CE can be used by people of all religions, Christians too. The year numbers are not changed.

Introducing Islam

This section tells you something about who Muslims are.

Muslims are followers of the religion of Islam. The words 'Muslim' and 'Islam' both come from an **Arabic** word which means **submission**. A Muslim is therefore someone who has submitted to God.

Islam began in the part of the world now called the Middle East. Many Muslims still live in this area, but today there are Muslims living in almost every country in the world.

What do Muslims believe?

Muslims believe that there is one God, whom they call **Allah**. They believe that Allah is **eternal**, which means he was never born and will never die. He made everything, knows everything and is all-powerful, so human beings must worship him.

Muslims believe that Allah sent **prophets** to teach people how to live. A prophet is someone who tells people what God wants. For Muslims, the last and most important prophet was a man called Muhammad. He lived in the country now called Saudi Arabia, and was born in 570 CE. Muslims believe that Muhammad received messages from Allah through the **Angel Jibril** (sometimes spelt Gabriel). These messages were collected together to form the Muslim holy book. This book is called the **Qur'an**.

Symbols for Islam

Muslims do not use **symbols** in the way that followers of some other religions do. When a symbol is needed for Islam, the one most often used is a star and crescent moon. This is found on many **mosques** and on the flags of some Muslim countries. The crescent moon is the new moon, and so is a symbol of the new lunar month. (The Muslim calendar follows the changes of the moon.) When the symbol is used on mosques, the crescent points in the direction of the city of Makkah. Makkah is a holy city for Muslims, and is where Muhammad was born.

Points to notice

There are two things which it is important to notice before you read any further.

- Muslims do not worship Muhammad. They believe that only Allah should be worshipped, and Muhammad was not Allah. However, Muhammad is given great respect as Allah's most important prophet and, to show this, whenever they mention

The star and crescent moon is sometimes used as a symbol for Islam

Arabic writing at the entrance to a mosque

Muhammad's name, Muslims add the words 'peace be upon him'. When written, this is sometimes shortened to 'pbuh'.

■ The language of Islam is Arabic. To be understood by people who cannot read it, Arabic words have to be changed into other alphabets. The sounds of letters in English are not the same as the sounds of Arabic letters, so sometimes different spellings are used. For example, Muhammad can be spelt Mahomet, and Makkah can be spelt Mecca. The spellings used in this book are those which give the sound closest to the original Arabic.

New words

Allah Arabic name for God, used by all Muslims

Angel Jibril messenger of Allah

Arabic language used in Muslim worship, and spoken by some Muslims

Eternal lasting for ever

Mosque Muslim place of worship

Muslim follower of the religion of Islam

Prophet someone who tells people what Allah wants

Qur'an Muslim holy book

Submission 'yield' – obey someone else's authority

Symbol something that stands for something else

Test yourself

What is the Arabic name for God?

Who was Muhammad?

What does 'submission' mean?

What's the Qur'an?

Things to do

1 Explain why Muslims believe that they should submit to Allah.

2 What do Muslims believe about Muhammad?

3 Draw the symbol which is often used for Islam. Explain why it is used.

4 Use an atlas or encyclopaedia to help you find out the names of three mainly Muslim countries.

The life of Muhammad

This section tells you something about Islam's most important prophet.

Muhammad was born in a city called Makkah, in what is today called Saudi Arabia. He was born in about the year 570 CE. Muhammad had a very hard childhood. His father died just before he was born. His mother died when he was only six years old. He was brought up by his grandfather and then his uncle. When he grew up, Muhammad helped his uncle in his work as a merchant.

As a young man, Muhammad was already well known for his honesty and goodness. He worked in Makkah for a wealthy woman called Khadijah. She was a trader. When Muhammad was 25, he and Khadijah were married. They were rich and respected, their marriage was very happy – it seemed that Muhammad had everything which he could possibly want.

However, he became more and more worried by the things which he saw going on in Makkah. It was a centre of trade, with many wealthy people. Muhammad saw rich merchants cheating the poor, and people spending their time gambling, drinking and fighting. **Idol** worship was common, and often included **sacrifices**. Muhammad was sure that these things were wrong. He felt that he needed to be alone to think, and began going to the mountains outside Makkah to **meditate**.

One night Muhammad was meditating in a cave on Mount Hira when he had a **vision**. In his vision, an angel came to him carrying a piece of cloth on which words were written. The angel said, 'Recite!' Muhammad said that he could not read. The angel repeated the command, and Muhammad found that he was able to understand the words and read them aloud. He stood up and walked out of the cave, and heard the angel saying, 'Muhammad! You are Allah's messenger!'

Muhammad was terrified by this experience. He returned home and told Khadijah about it, and she comforted him, and was the first person to believe his message came from Allah. Muhammad began preaching to people in Makkah, but he became unpopular. Although a few people believed what Muhammad was telling them, most of the people did not like being told they were wicked sinners. Many people were against him, so in 622 CE Muhammad accepted an invitation from the people in the nearby town of Madinah. They had heard about his preaching, and asked him to go and teach them.

Makkah and Mount Hira today

The Mosque of the Prophet in Madinah

The hijrah

Muhammad's move to Madinah is called the **hijrah**. This is an Arabic word which means 'departure'. Muslims think that this is very important, because it was the beginning of the success of Islam. The Muslim calendar begins from this date, and years are numbered AH which means 'the year of the hijrah'.

While Muhammad was living in Madinah, there were battles with the people of Makkah. This was because Muhammad was trying to stop people doing things that were wrong. At last, the people of Makkah were defeated and Muhammad returned in triumph. The Makkans accepted Islam as their religion, and all the idols and statues were taken out of the city. Muhammad returned to Madinah, and spent the rest of his life teaching the people there. He died in 632 CE, and was buried in his house in Madinah. The Mosque of the Prophet now extends over his grave.

New words

Hijrah departure – name given to Muhammad's journey to Madinah
Idol statue worshipped as a god
Meditate to think deeply, especially about religion
Sacrifice offering made to a god

Test yourself

Where was Muhammad born?

Who was Khadijah?

What does 'hijrah' mean?

Where did Muhammad die?

Things to do

1 Muhammad was rich and respected in Makkah. Why do you think he gave up everything to preach about Allah?

2 How many reasons can you think of why Muhammad's preaching was not accepted by the people of Makkah?

3 Explain why Muslims think that Muhammad's departure from Makkah was so important.

4 Imagine what it must have been like when Muhammad received the vision of the Angel Jibril. Write an article describing how he might have felt.

5 Working in small groups, put together a short play which shows what it might have been like when Muhammad returned to Makkah in triumph.

The Qur'an

This section tells you about the Qur'an, the Muslims' holy book.

Muslims believe that the words of the Qur'an are the words of Allah. They were given to Muhammad by the Angel Jibril. The word Qur'an means **recitation** and Muslims believe that Muhammad recited what the Angel Jibril taught him. He then taught several of his friends, and they too learned the words by heart. Muhammad could not read or write, but the friends who had learned it wrote it down. The Qur'an was written down in one book within twenty years of Muhammad's death.

Muslims believe that the words of the Qur'an should not be changed in any way, because they are the words of Allah. Muslims who do not speak Arabic may have a translation into their own language for their own use, but for worship the Qur'an is always read in Arabic. All Muslims can recite parts of the Qur'an in Arabic.

Copies of the Qur'an are treated with great respect. When a copy is not being used, it is kept carefully wrapped on the highest piece of furniture in the room. Before reading it, a Muslim will wash, or sometimes have a bath. The Qur'an is often placed on a stand to be read, so that it does not have to be handled too much. Some Muslims learn the whole of the Qur'an by heart, because they believe that what it teaches is so important. Those who succeed in doing this are allowed to use the title **hafiz** as part of their name.

Contents of the Qur'an

The Qur'an is made up of 114 chapters, which are called surahs. These are of different lengths. The longest is surah 2, which has 286 verses, the shortest is surah 103 which has only three verses. Except for surah 9, they all begin with the words 'In the name of Allah, most

This girl is reading the Qur'an

gracious, most merciful'. Some surahs describe events, others give teaching. The teaching is very detailed, and Muslims believe that it is important because it tells them how they should live.

The Qur'an does not say that Muhammad was Allah's only prophet. It accepts that people who are important in the teachings of **Judaism** and **Christianity** were prophets, too. For example, Abraham (Muslims call him Ibrahim), Moses (Musa) and Jesus (Isa) are all mentioned in the Qur'an. According to the Qur'an, the problem was that even though they had the teachings of these prophets, people kept forgetting what Allah was like. Allah called Muhammad to be his prophet, and gave him the Qur'an so that people would not forget his teachings. Muslims believe that the **scriptures** of other religions were given by God, but they have been altered by human beings. Only the Qur'an has been kept in its original form and so is truly the word of Allah. In other words, Muslims believe that Islam completes what Judaism and Christianity began.

The Hadith

For Muslims, the **Hadith** is the other important collection of teachings. The books of the Hadith contain the collected sayings of Muhammad. They are still used today to advise Muslims on how to act. A Muslim with a problem – not just in their faith, but in any area of their life – will look in the Hadith to find out what Muhammad said or did in the same or a similar situation.

This is the first surah in a decorated copy of the Qur'an

New words

Christianity religion of Christians
Hadith teachings based on the life of Muhammad
Hafiz person who has learned the Qur'an by heart
Judaism religion of the Jews
Recitation repeating something learned by heart
Scriptures holy books
Surah chapter in the Qur'an

Test yourself

What's the Qur'an?

Who uses the title 'hafiz'?

What's a surah?

What's the Hadith?

Things to do

1 List three things which tell you that Muslims think the Qur'an is very important.

2 Explain what the Qur'an teaches about Judaism and Christianity.

3 Why do you think that Muslims use the Hadith to guide them in their lives?

4 Find out some of the teachings of the Qur'an. (If you can't find a copy of the Qur'an itself, your school or local library will have some books which include quotations from it.) Work in groups and when you have written out the teachings, put them together to make a wall display. If you use drawings to illustrate them, remember that Muslims never draw pictures of people or animals.

The Mosque

This section tells you about the place where Muslims go to worship.

Muslims believe that they can worship Allah anywhere, and they do not have to be in a special building. However, like members of most other religions, many Muslims feel that it is important to have a special place for worship. This place is called a mosque. (The Arabic name 'masjid' is sometimes used instead.) Many Muslim men go to the mosque several times a week, but the most important time is the lunch-time prayers on a Friday, the Muslim holy day. Women are expected to pray too, either at the mosque or at home. When they go to the mosque, they stay separate from the men. Muslims believe that this allows both men and women to concentrate on Allah.

A mosque usually has a **dome** and at least one tall tower called a **minaret**. From the top of this tower, the **adhan** is called five times a day. This is the call to prayer, and many mosques have loudspeakers so that the adhan can be heard clearly.

An essential part of all mosques is a supply of water. Sometimes this is in a courtyard with a pool or fountain, sometimes it is in a cloakroom. It is needed because all Muslims wash before they pray. This is a special washing, explained on page 16, which has nothing to do with being dirty. Muslims also take off their shoes before they go into the mosque, to show respect and keep the mosque clean for prayer.

Inside a mosque

Many mosques are beautifully decorated. There are never any pictures or statues, because Muhammad said that these should be avoided in case people began to worship them. The decorations are made with cleverly designed patterns and verses from the Qur'an. Often the verses are made into patterns, too.

There are no seats in a mosque, but the floor is carpeted or has special prayer mats. When they pray, Muslims always face Makkah, so mosques have a small arch in one wall which shows the exact direction of Makkah. This is called the **mihrab**. There is also a raised platform which is usually at the top of a short flight of steps. This is called the **minbar**. It is used by the **imam** when he preaches on a Friday. The imam is a leader who is chosen by other Muslims because he knows the Qur'an well. Being an imam is not always the man's full-time job, and he is not always paid. Preaching in a mosque is based on the Qur'an. The imam explains its teachings and talks about life as a Muslim.

A mosque in Birmingham

Inside Regent's Park mosque in London (notice the mihrab at the front)

Mosques are used for prayers every day, and they are also used for other things to do with the religion. For example, in Britain, many Muslim children go to the mosque after school to learn about Islam and the Qur'an, because they are not taught much about them at school.

New words

Adhan call to prayer
Dome roof shaped like half a ball
Imam Muslim leader and teacher
Mihrab arch in the wall which shows the direction of Makkah
Minaret tower of a mosque
Minbar platform used for preaching

Test yourself

What's a mosque?

What's a minaret?

Where does the mihrab face?

What's an imam?

Things to do

1 Why is there always water available in a mosque? (Looking at the section on worship, page 16, may help.)

2 Why do you think Muslims believe that it is important for their children to learn about Islam and the Qur'an?

3 Mosques are usually very beautiful buildings. How many reasons can you think of why this should be so?

4 If possible, try to arrange a visit to a mosque in your area. If this is not possible, find out as much as you can about mosques, and work in groups to prepare a project with drawings or a model.

The five pillars of Islam

This section tells you about the most important parts of Muslim worship.

There are five most important parts to Muslim worship. They are called the five pillars of Islam. A pillar is something which supports a building, so the five pillars of Islam 'support' the religion. Muslims believe that following the five pillars helps them to keep their religion properly.

The first pillar – Shahadah

Shahadah is the declaration of faith. In other words, it is a summing up of the most important part of Muslim belief. It is usually translated into English as 'There is no other god but Allah, and Muhammad is the prophet of Allah.'

These words form part of the adhan, the call to prayer (see page 12). They are whispered into the ear of newborn babies, so that they are the first words they hear. A Muslim who is still able to speak will repeat them as they are dying. They are the first words which a Muslim says on waking up, and the last they say before going to sleep.

The second pillar – Salat

Salat means prayer five times a day. Muslims pray early in the morning, at night and on three occasions during the day. Male Muslims are expected to go to the mosque for the noon prayers on a Friday, but otherwise they pray in any clean place. When it is time for prayer, Muslims stop whatever they are doing, and face in the direction of Makkah. (The positions for prayers are described on pages 16–17.) In Muslim countries, a **mu'adhin** calls the people to prayer from the mosque. (Mu'adhin is sometimes written 'muezzin'.) He recites the adhan, and adds, 'Come to prayer, come to security, Allah is most great!' In the morning, he adds the words 'Prayer is better than sleep!'

The third pillar – Zakah

'Zakah' means giving money to people who are poor or in need. Every year, Muslims are expected to give a certain amount of their money to charity. This can be used for things like building hospitals as well as direct help for poorer Muslims. This money is called Zakah (sometimes Zakat). It amounts to about 2.5 per cent of the money which a Muslim has received

The five pillars

FAITH PRAYER ALMS FASTING PILGRIMAGE

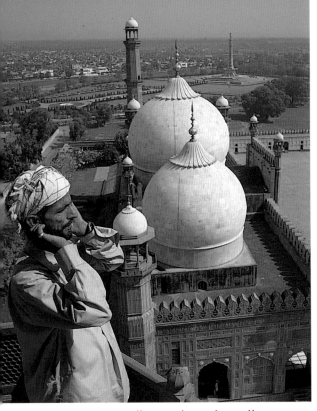

A mu'adhin making the call to prayer

New words

Fasting doing without food and drink for religious reasons

Mu'adhin man who calls Muslims to prayer

Pilgrimage journey for religious reasons

Test yourself

What's the adhan?

What's a mu'adhin?

When do Muslims fast?

What's Hajj?

Things to do

1 Explain what the five pillars of Islam are. Why do they have this name?

2 Make your own diagram to show Islam as a building supported by the five pillars.

3 The morning call to prayer says that 'Prayer is better than sleep!' What do you think Muslims mean when they say this?

4 What sort of things could money given to charity be spent on? Work in groups to discuss your ideas, then collect a list.

and not spent in a year. It does not include money which is spent on necessary things like food and clothes. Zakah is thought of as being an offering to Allah, so all Muslims are expected to give it. Not to give Zakah would mean that they were not doing their duty to poorer Muslims, and – even more important – it would mean that they were cheating Allah.

The fourth pillar – Sawm

Sawm is **fasting** during the month of Ramadan. Ramadan is the ninth month of the Muslim year. During this month, most Muslims do not eat or drink during the hours of daylight. They try hard to live especially good lives. (This is explained in more detail on page 22.)

The fifth pillar – Hajj

Hajj is **pilgrimage** to Makkah. Every Muslim who can afford it is expected to visit Makkah at least once during their life. For Muslims, Makkah is a most holy place, because it is where Muhammad lived and worked. (Hajj is explained in more detail on pages 18–21.)

Muslim worship

This section tells you about how Muslims worship.

The most important part of Muslim worship is prayer. Prayer five times a day is the second of the five pillars of Islam. Muslims always pray facing towards Makkah. In a mosque, there is a special arch in the wall to show the direction to face. For prayers when they are not in a mosque, Muslims can carry a special compass. Using this, they can work out the position of Makkah from anywhere in the world. If the floor is not clean, Muslims use a special mat for prayers. After the set prayers, Muslims may use a string of 33 or 99 beads to allow them to remember Allah 99 times. There are 99 names for Allah in the Qur'an – the wise, the merciful, etc. Some Muslims count with the finger joints of their right hand instead of using beads.

The times of prayers are laid down in the Qur'an. The first prayers should be between first light and sunrise, the second after the sun has left the highest point in the sky. The third prayers should be between mid-afternoon and sunset, the fourth between sunset and darkness. The fifth prayers of the day are between darkness and first light. In Muslim countries, the people are reminded that it is time to pray by the mu'adhin who calls them to prayer from the mosque.

Wudu

Before praying, Muslims wash. This is a special washing, called **wudu**, and has nothing to do with being dirty. If they are actually dirty, Muslims bath completely before praying. Wudu is intended to make the person fit to worship Allah, who is holy. It gives them time to forget what they were doing, and get ready to concentrate on Allah. Some Muslims prefer to use cold water for washing, so that they are more alert, especially at the morning prayers.

Washing is always done in the same order, to make sure that nothing is forgotten. The instructions for how it should be done are in the Qur'an. First, the right hand is washed, to the wrist. Then the left hand in the same way. Next, the mouth and throat, by gargling, so that the voice is clean to talk to Allah. Then the nose and face are washed, and the right arm up to the elbow, then the left. The head is wiped with a wet hand, then the ears are cleaned. Finally, the feet are washed up to the ankles, right one first. If no water is available, clean sand or earth may be used instead.

Rak'ahs

When a Muslim prays, they do not just make up prayers, although there is opportunity for private prayer. The prayers follow a set pattern called a **rak'ah**. Two rak'ahs are made at morning prayers, four at midday and in the afternoon, three in the evening and four at night.

A rak'ah includes several different positions. The Muslim stands, bows, kneels and touches the ground with the forehead. Different parts of the prayer are said in each position.

Wudu is the special washing before prayer

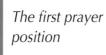

The first prayer position

The position for making personal prayers

The following description is of a man praying, but women pray in the same way.

The first movement shows that he intends to pray. In the second, he repeats the first verses of the Qur'an ('You alone do we worship ...'.) In positions three to eight, he praises Allah for his goodness. In the ninth movement, he prays for Muhammad and all Muslims everywhere. He turns his head from side to side, to greet the two angels whom Muslims believe are always with every person, though they cannot be seen.

At the end of the set prayer, the Muslim can add his own private prayers if he wishes. These are called **du'a**. He stays in a kneeling position, with his hands palm upwards. Some Muslims wipe their hand over their face as a sign that they have finished their prayers. Du'a can be made at any time, as well as at the end of a rak'ah.

New words

Du'a personal prayers
Rak'ah set of positions for Muslim prayers
Wudu special washing before prayer

Test yourself

How many times a day do Muslims pray?

Where do Muslims face when they pray?

What's wudu?

What's a rak'ah?

Things to do

1 Explain why washing before prayer is important to Muslims.

2 How do you think the positions for prayers help to show that Muslims have submitted to Allah?

3 What advantages and disadvantages can you think of for having five prayer times every day?

4 Find out more about what Muslims believe about the two angels who are always with every person (page 47 will help). How do you think this belief might affect the way that Muslims live?

The Hajj I

This section tells you about how Muslims prepare for pilgrimage to Makkah.

Hajj – pilgrimage to Makkah – is the fifth of the five pillars of Islam. Every Muslim who has the health and wealth is expected to go to Makkah at least once during their life. Many people save up for years until they can afford it, and often families join together to pay for one person to go. Every year, about two million Muslims travel from all over the world to make Hajj. For each of them, it is a very special journey, and one which they will remember all their lives.

To be a true Hajj, the pilgrimage must take place between 8 and 13 Dhul-Hijjah, the last month of the Muslim year. Of course Muslims can go to Makkah at other times, but the pilgrimage is then called **Umrah**, and is not so important. Today, there are so many Muslims wanting to go for Hajj that Muslims who have been before are encouraged to go at other times of the year. Non-Muslims are not allowed into the holy city of Makkah.

Ihram

Ihram is the word given to the special state in which pilgrims are expected to live whilst they are on Hajj. They are expected to live pure lives, and are not supposed to swear or quarrel. Any sexual relationship is forbidden, even if husbands and wives are together. As a sign of the purity of the thoughts of all pilgrims, women are not allowed to cover their faces, even if they do so in their normal life.

The pilgrim camp

All male pilgrims wear exactly the same clothes, two sheets of white cotton which do not have any seams. One sheet covers the lower half of their body, the other is worn over the left shoulder. These clothes are also called 'ihram'. They are worn so that everyone looks alike, and it does not matter whether they are old or young, rich or poor. It is a sign that everyone is equal before Allah. Men may not cover their heads, although they are allowed to carry an umbrella to protect themselves from the heat of the sun. Women do not wear special clothes, but they wear head-veils, and make sure that everything they wear is simple. Pilgrims should go barefoot, or wear only open sandals. To add to the simplicity, no-one wears jewellery or perfume or uses scented soap. Hair and nails are not trimmed during Hajj.

Men who have completed the Hajj can be called Hajji, women Hajjah. For every pilgrim, Hajj is a very joyful time. They share worship with thousands of other pilgrims, but the point of the Hajj is that for each pilgrim, it is an individual experience.

The purpose of Hajj is to 'meet' Allah. Muslims believe that if Hajj is properly performed in the right frame of mind a pilgrim can gain forgiveness for everything they have done wrong in their life.

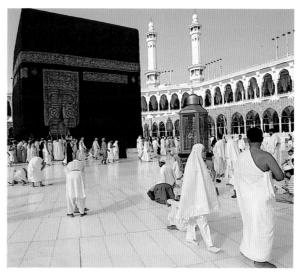

Pilgrims wearing ihram

Test yourself

What's Hajj?

When does Hajj take place?

Where do pilgrims go for Hajj?

Things to do

1 What are the special clothes which pilgrims wear? Why do they wear them?

2 a How are pilgrims on Hajj expected to live?

  b What effect do you think this has on the pilgrimage?

  c How would it change the world if people lived all the time without swearing or quarrelling?

3 What do Muslims believe can happen if Hajj is performed properly? Explain why this means that making Hajj is so important for Muslims.

New words

Hajj pilgrimage to Makkah
Ihram special way of living for Hajj (also the special clothes)
Umrah 'lesser pilgrimage'

The Hajj II

This section tells you about how Muslims perform the Hajj.

Most pilgrims sail or fly to start the pilgrimage at Jeddah, then travel on to Makkah by bus or car. When they reach Makkah, they go first to the Great Mosque which contains the **Ka'bah**.

The Ka'bah is a cube-shaped building 15 metres long, 10 metres wide and 14 metres high. Inside it is a room which is decorated with parts of the Qur'an. Muslims believe that the Ka'bah is the oldest place of worship of Allah, since it was built by Adam, the first man. It is covered by a black cloth which is beautifully embroidered with the words of the Qur'an. This cloth is replaced every year, because at the end of each Hajj it is cut into pieces which are given to pilgrims to take home as a reminder of the pilgrimage. In one corner of the Ka'bah is the black stone. Muslims believe that this was given to Ibrahim's son, Isma'il, by the Angel Jibril. Every pilgrim walks or runs round the Ka'bah seven times. Those who are close enough touch it or kiss it. Those further away raise their hands towards it.

Pilgrims walk round the Ka'bah

After they have done this, the pilgrims go to pray near the Maqam Ibrahim (Ibrahim's place) which is close to the Ka'bah. Then they hurry seven times between two small hills not far from the Ka'bah. This remembers how Ibrahim's wife, Hajar ran between these two hills looking for water for her baby son Isma'il. Today the hills are linked by a broad corridor. The spring which Muslims believe Isma'il found when he dug his toes in the sand is now called the Well of Zamzam, and is in the courtyard of the Great Mosque. Pilgrims drink water from this well, and often collect some of the water to take home for family and friends.

The ninth day of the month is usually the second or third day of the pilgrimage, and the pilgrims travel to the Plain of Arafat, which is about 20 kilometres from Makkah. They travel there to 'stand before Allah' – **wuquf**. They ask Allah to forgive all their **sins**, the wrong things which they have done in their life. The pilgrims stand from midday until sunset, thinking about Allah and praying. This is the most important part of the pilgrimage, and without it the Hajj is not complete. Then they travel back to Muzdalifah in time for the evening prayers, and camp there overnight.

The corridor which links the two hills

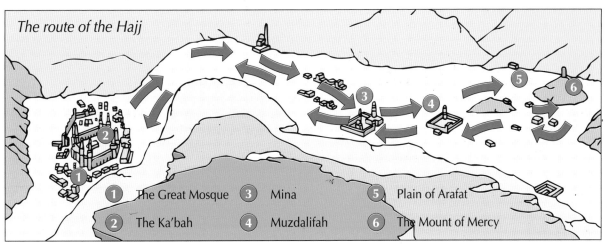

The route of the Hajj

① The Great Mosque		③ Mina		⑤ Plain of Arafat	
② The Ka'bah		④ Muzdalifah		⑥ The Mount of Mercy	

On the morning of the tenth day, the pilgrims go to Mina, where there are three stone pillars. Pilgrims throw stones at these seven times, to remember how Ibrahim and his family drove away the **Devil** who was tempting them. After the first pillar has been stoned, many pilgrims sacrifice an animal, usually a sheep or a goat. This is part of the festival of Id ul Adha, which is celebrated by Muslims all over the world. Male pilgrims then either shave their heads or cut their hair and women cut off a lock of their hair. They do this because it is what Muhammad did. Then they take off the special pilgrim clothes, and put on their normal clothes. The pilgrims camp at Mina for three days, after which they travel back to Makkah, and walk around the Ka'bah again. They drink as much water as they can from the Well of Zamzam. Then the Hajj is ended and the pilgrims can travel home if they wish. In fact, many choose to stay for longer, and visit other important places in the area – for example, the Mosque of the Prophet and Muhammad's tomb at Madinah.

Test yourself

Where's the Ka'bah?

Who found the Well of Zamzam?

What's wuquf?

Things to do

1 Draw the Ka'bah. Write a paragraph explaining what it is, and why it is so important to Muslims.

2 Why do you think pilgrims bring back water from the Well of Zamzam for people at home?

3 Using the map and the text to help you, write an outline of what happens on each day of Hajj.

4 If possible, interview a Muslim who is Hajji or Hajjah. Ask what they remember most about Hajj, and how they feel about their pilgrimage.

New words

Devil spirit of evil
Ka'bah most important place of Muslim worship
Sins 'wrong-doing' – something which separates a person from God
Wuquf 'stand before Allah' – most important part of Hajj

Ramadan

This section tells you about an important Muslim celebration.

Every year, during the month called Ramadan, Muslims fast during the hours of daylight. The custom of fasting in Ramadan goes back to the time of Muhammad. He taught his followers that the fast was important, because it was a sign that they had submitted to Allah. Fasting like this is very hard, but Muslims believe that it teaches them to have patience, and not to give up just because things are difficult. It also reminds them that their religion is the most important thing in their lives, far more important than food and drink. One of the aims of Ramadan is to make everyone equal, because hunger is the same for everyone, whether they are rich or poor. At the end of a successful Ramadan, a Muslim feels much more able to face up to any problems which life brings.

Prayers at a mosque in Istanbul

During Ramadan, all eating must finish before dawn, so the day begins well before this. To make sure that there is no confusion about what time fasting should begin or end, special lists are published showing the times of dawn and sunset in different places. The first meal is not usually a large one, but it contains foods which will give energy for the day. Then the Muslim's life goes on as normal, except that they eat and drink nothing. At sunset, they have a light snack, followed later by a main meal.

It is very difficult to eat and drink nothing all day, especially in hot countries. Sometimes it may get too much, and a person may feel that they must eat or drink. If a Muslim breaks the fast without a good reason, he or she should fast for an extra 60 days. Ramadan is intended to be difficult, but it is not intended to be cruel. Therefore exceptions are made, and not all Muslims are expected to fast. The very old and the young (usually children under the age of twelve) are excused. People who are on a journey may eat while they are travelling, but should make up the extra days of fasting later. Anyone who is ill is not expected to fast, and neither is a woman who is pregnant. They are expected to make up the missed days when they are healthy. If someone has a health problem which means they can never fast, they are expected to pay a sum of money which would buy a meal for 60 people.

Although these things are expected of Muslims, whether or not they do them is up to each individual's conscience. There are no punishments if they do not keep the fast. Muslims believe that the judge of someone's behaviour is Allah, who knows everything and sees everything. At the end of the world, Allah will judge everyone on how they have lived, and each person will get what they deserve.

A Muslim family in Britain breaking their fast

The point is that if they fail to keep to what their religion expects, they are cheating not only themselves, but Allah, too. Muhammad taught that everyone who fasts will get two rewards. They will get the joy of being able to eat again when the fast has finished, and they will also be rewarded by Allah at the **Day of Judgement.**

As well as fasting, Muslims try to live especially pure lives during Ramadan. They do not smoke, or have sexual relationships during the day. They spend extra time on religious matters. They are expected to attend special prayers, and they spend more time reading the Qur'an. Many Muslims try to read all the way through the Qur'an during the month. Some Muslims choose to go and stay in the mosque during the last ten days of Ramadan. This is called a **retreat.** They take only a few necessary possessions with them, and live simply, reading the Qur'an and praying and thinking about spiritual matters. They do this because it is how Muhammad spent the last part of Ramadan when he was alive, so they believe that they are following his example. The month of Ramadan ends with the festival of Id-ul-Fitr.

New words

Day of Judgement the end of the world, when Allah will judge everyone

Retreat special time of praying and thinking

Test yourself

When do Muslims fast?

When's the Day of Judgement?

What's a retreat?

Things to do

1 Explain why Muslims believe that fasting during Ramadan is so important.

2 Apart from fasting, what makes Ramadan a special month? What differences do you think it makes to a Muslim's life when they spend a month like this?

3 Do you think it is a good idea to leave it to someone's conscience how they keep Ramadan? Does it make it more or less likely that they will keep it carefully?

4 List all the things you ate and drank between dawn and sunset yesterday. Then write an article about how you think you would feel if you were fasting for the 29 or 30 days of Ramadan.

Id-ul-Fitr and Id-ul-Adha

This section tells you about two important Muslim festivals.

Id-ul-Fitr

Id-ul-Fitr is the festival which ends Ramadan. It begins on the first day of the tenth month of the Muslim year. It marks the end of the difficult month of fasting, so it is looked forward to very much. Before the festival begins, Muslims observe Zakat-ul-Fitr. This means giving money for the poor. Usually the amount given is what it costs to buy a meal for a family. The idea is that everyone should have enough money to celebrate the feast, no matter how poor they are.

On the last night of Ramadan, many people do not bother to go to bed. Instead, they meet outside to watch for the new moon. When the moon can be seen, the new month of Shawwal has begun, and so the festival can start.

Id cards

Gifts for Id

The first day of the festival begins with a light meal. Then Muslims meet at the mosque. Id-ul-Fitr is a time for meeting friends and relatives, so it is common for large groups to meet at the mosque for prayers. The special prayers take place between dawn and noon, and Muslims give thanks for a successful fast. After the prayers, families and friends meet in each other's homes. Id is a time when people who have not seen each other for a long time can meet and talk. There are parties, especially for children, and people give each other presents. Children often wear new clothes. Special cakes and sugary sweets are eaten. Many Muslims also celebrate Id by sending greeting cards to each other. A common greeting is 'Id mubarak' – 'Id blessings!'

Id-ul-Adha

The festival of Id-ul-Adha takes place in the month of Dhul-Hijjah. It is celebrated by Muslims all over the world, although it is especially important for Muslims who are on the Hajj, the pilgrimage to Makkah. They celebrate the festival at Mina.

The name Id-ul-Adha means 'Feast of Sacrifice'. It is the festival at which Muslims remember that Ibrahim was ready to make a sacrifice of his son, Isma'il. He did not have to do this, because just in time he heard a voice telling him that he should sacrifice a ram instead. However, the point of the story is that Ibrahim was ready to give up the most important thing in his life – his son – because he believed it was what Allah wanted.

On the morning of 10 Dhul-Hijjah, Muslims may sacrifice an animal. Usually this is a sheep or a goat, though other larger animals are sometimes used, especially if families join together to make the sacrifice. Sacrificing the animal is a symbol. Its life is being given to Allah, and this is a sign that Muslims themselves are ready to give up everything for Allah.

Like any animal which a Muslim is to eat, the animal sacrificed at Id-ul-Adha is killed in a special way. All the blood is drained away, and it becomes **halal**. 'Halal' means 'allowed' so halal meat is meat which Muslims are allowed to eat. (This is explained in more detail on pages 40–41.) The meat from the sacrificed animal is shared out, and one third of it is always given to the poor.

Like Id-ul-Fitr, Muslims celebrate the rest of the festival with family and friends, and by exchanging presents. Id-ul-Adha is a longer and more important festival than Id-ul-Fitr.

New word

Halal 'allowed' – food which Muslims can eat

Test yourself

When is Id-ul-Fitr?

What does 'Zakat-ul-Fitr' mean?

What does 'halal' mean?

Things to do

1 Why do Muslims look forward to Id-ul-Fitr so much?

2 All Muslims are expected to give to people who are poorer than themselves. Why do you think this is such an important part of what Islam teaches?

3 Design a card which would be suitable to send to a Muslim at Id-ul-Fitr.

4 Imagine that you are a Muslim child at Id-ul-Fitr. Write an entry for your diary on the first night of the festival. You could include how you spent the day, and how you feel about the end of Ramadan and the beginning of the festival.

5 Look up Genesis 22 : 1–13 in a Bible (the Christian holy book). How does this show that Islam, Judaism and Christianity share the same history?

The minor celebrations

This section tells you about some of the days of celebration in the Muslim year.

The Day of the Hijrah (1 Muharram)

Muharram is the first month of the Muslim year, so 1 Muharram is New Year's Day in the Muslim calendar. It is also important for another reason. It is the day on which Muslims remember the journey which Muhammad made from Makkah to Madinah. They believe that this was a very important event, because it was after this that Islam became important as a religion. Therefore, 1 Muharram is not just the day which marks the beginning of the new year, it is also the day on which Muslims remember the beginning of the success of Islam. Many Muslims make New Year's Resolutions on this day, believing that they are leaving behind their old ways in the same way that Muhammad left Makkah.

The Dome of the Rock mosque in Jerusalem

The Prophet's birthday (12 Rabi al-Awwal)

Muhammad's birthday was on the twelfth day of the third month of the year, which is called Rabi al-Awwal. Some Muslims celebrate this as a special day, because of their love for Muhammad, and because they believe he was the last and most important of all the prophets. During this month Muslims may meet to remember events in Muhammad's life. Many Muslims do not agree with attaching this much importance to the birth of a human being, and so do not approve of the celebrations.

The Night of Power (27 Ramadan)

This festival remembers the night when Muhammad first received the Qur'an from the Angel Jibril. It falls during the last part of the month of Ramadan. Most Muslims celebrate it on 27 Ramadan, although the exact date on which it occurred is not known. Many Muslims spend extra time reading the Qur'an at this time, and thinking about its importance in their lives.

The Night of the Journey (27 Rajab)

Muslims believe that on the night of 27 Rajab, Muhammad made an amazing journey from Makkah to Jerusalem. (Some Muslims believe that it was a vision rather than something which really happened.) From Jerusalem, Muhammad was taken up to heaven, and heard Allah telling him to teach his followers about the importance of prayer five times a day. The most important mosque in Jerusalem, the Mosque of the Dome of the Rock, is built at the place from which it is said that Muhammad was taken up to heaven.

The celebrations for the different festivals are not the same, but they are all times when families and friends can get together. This can be very important, especially when people do not live as close to their relatives as they used to. Muslims believe strongly that festivals should be times of happiness and friendship where everyone is involved.

Test yourself

When is the Muslim New Year?

What happened on the Night of Power?

Where's the Dome of the Rock?

Things to do

1 Explain why 1 Muharram is such an important day for Muslims.

2 In the Qur'an, the night when the Qur'an was given to Muhammad is called the Night of Power. What do you think this name suggests?

3 Working in groups, put together a short play which would be suitable for an entertainment celebrating the Prophet's birthday. (Remember that Muslims would never include anyone playing the part of Muhammad.)

4 Find out more about how Muslims celebrate one of these festivals. Talk to a Muslim if possible. If not, books from your school or local library should help. Write an article about the celebration of the festival you have chosen.

The history of Islam

This section tells you something about the history of Islam.

After Muhammad died, the area of land which Muslims ruled grew quite quickly. Muhammad had taught that fighting was not wrong if it was to defeat persecution. Trying to overcome any sort of evil is called **jihad**, which means 'to struggle'. It is an important part of Muslim belief. This can mean that fighting battles is permitted, if there is no other way. The men who took over from Muhammad as leaders of Islam fought to make Islam grow stronger. Their first task was to conquer the groups which had left Islam when Muhammad died. When they had done this, groups further away began to attack, but the Muslims defeated them. Within a hundred years they ruled a very large area.

Over the next few hundred years, Muslims came to rule more and more parts of the world. They went east, and much of India became Muslim. Muslim leaders were in power there until the middle of the nineteenth century. They went west, through the north of Africa, and crossed the Mediterranean Sea into Spain. They went north and, over several hundred years, gained power in a large part of eastern Europe.

One of the areas where most battles were fought was the land at the eastern end of the Mediterranean Sea. This was the area called Palestine. It is important to Muslims, but it is also important to Jews and to Christians. Jewish and Christian soldiers fought Muslim soldiers over the land for many years. At this time in the Middle Ages holy wars known as the Crusades were fought. Many battles were fought around the city of Jerusalem, because all three religions believe that this is a holy city, and all three wanted to control it. The Muslims were generally better fighters. Where they took control, they allowed the Christians and Jews to continue to follow their own religions, but they had to pay a special tax. This was instead of serving in the Muslim army, which people who had been conquered would normally have been expected to do.

Muslim rule in 732 CE

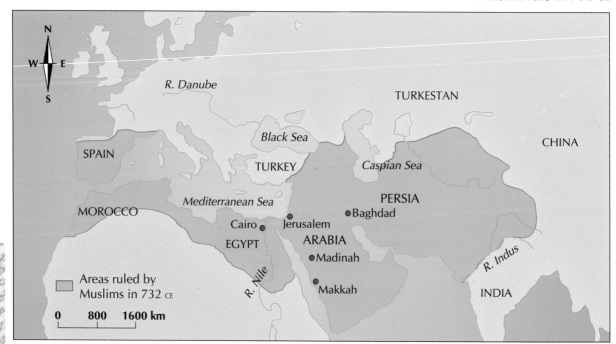

28

The Alhambra in Spain was built by Muslims

One of the most important Muslim nations was called the Ottoman Empire. It was most powerful between about 400 CE and 1600 CE. After this time it lost some of its land, but it did not finally end until after the end of World War I in 1918. One of its most famous rulers was Suleiman the Magnificent, who ruled from 1520 to 1566.

Islam did not just spread by fighting. Many Muslims were traders, and they travelled all over the world buying and selling goods. Where they travelled, they took their religion with them. They became well known for the fact that they lived good lives, and people respected them. Sometimes the people they met were so impressed that they decided they would become Muslims too, and gradually Islam spread.

Today, there are about 1000 million followers of Islam, and there are Muslims living in most countries of the world. About 1.5 million Muslims live in Britain. Islam is growing faster than any other religion.

New word

Jihad struggle against evil

Test yourself

When were the Crusades?

When did the Ottoman Empire have most power?

Roughly how many Muslims are there in the world today?

Things to do

1 Explain why Jews, Christians and Muslims all wanted to control Palestine.

2 Working in groups, discuss the advantages and disadvantages of spreading a religion by:
a fighting about it
b impressing people by your life.

3 Find out about someone in the news who is standing up for what they believe. Write a letter to an imaginary newspaper saying why you agree or disagree with the stand being taken.

4 How many reasons can you think of why Islam has spread throughout the world?

Modern Islam

This section tells you about the two main groups of Muslims today.

Muhammad and his followers were called Muslims because they had submitted to the will of Allah. Whilst Muhammad was alive, he had the greatest authority among his friends. If there were any arguments, they would ask Muhammad for his advice, and he would sort out the problem. After Muhammad died, his friends decided that they needed a new leader. They decided that the 'best' Muslim should be chosen. They agreed that this man was Abu Bakr. Abu Bakr had been one of Muhammad's closest friends. Now he became a leader called a **khalifah**. After Abu Bakr, three other khalifahs led the Muslims in turn. They were Umar, Uthman and Ali. Ali was married to Muhammad's daughter. These khalifahs were all chosen by the rest of the group.

About 50 years after Muhammad had died, some Muslims came to have different opinions about how khalifahs should be chosen. They began to feel that rather than being chosen by other Muslims, khalifahs should be members of Muhammad's family. Muhammad's sons had died when they were children, so they believed the first khalifah should have been Ali, Muhammad's son-in-law. The next should have been Ali's son, and so on. The disagreement became more and more bitter, until the Muslims who supported Ali's family split away into a separate group. They are called Shi'ah Muslims. About ten per cent of Muslims in the world today belong to this group.

Shi'ah Muslims

Most Shi'ah Muslims live in Iran and Iraq. Many Shi'ahs are very strict about what they believe and are often more extreme in their views. It is part of Muslim belief that anyone who is a **martyr** will go straight to Allah and live in **Paradise**. A martyr is someone who dies for their faith. The fact that they believe this means that Muslims are sometimes ready to give up their life in fighting for what they believe is right. This is one reason why Shi'ah Muslims are often in the news.

Countries where over 50 per cent of the people are Muslim

30

Shi'ah Muslims

Muslims believe that they need teachers to help them understand what the Qur'an means. All Muslim teachers are called 'imams', but Shi'ahs believe that there were twelve imams who were given special power by Allah, just as Muhammad was. They believe that the first imam was Ali, who was chosen by Muhammad. His power was passed on from father to son until the last imam, who disappeared in 880 CE. Shi'ahs believe that he will return one day and, until he does, his teachings are in the hands of 'doctors of the law'. The most important of these leaders are called **Ayatollahs**.

Sunni Muslims

When the Shi'ahs split away, a much bigger group of Muslims was left behind. This group became the Sunni Muslims. The word 'Sunni' comes from an Arabic word which means

'authority', and Sunnis think of themselves as the true followers of Muhammad's teachings. Today about 90 per cent of Muslims belong to the Sunnis. The main difference between Sunni and Shi'ah belief is that the Sunnis accept the first four khalifahs as the true leaders of Islam, but Shi'ahs only accept Ali and his sons. They also have different opinions about what some parts of the Qur'an mean. Over many years, Sunnis as well as Shi'ahs gradually developed laws to make sure that the teachings of the Qur'an were followed. These laws have become the national laws for Muslim countries.

Test yourself

What's a khalifah?

What's a martyr?

How many Muslims are Sunnis?

Things to do

1 Explain why Shi'ah Muslims split away from Sunni Muslims.

2 Why do you think some Muslims are prepared to die for their beliefs?

3 What does the word 'Sunni' come from? Why do you think the group chose this name for themselves?

4 Make a scrapbook about Islam in the world today. You could use cuttings from newspapers and magazines, and you may be able to use pictures from travel agents' books. Egypt and Tunisia are countries where many Muslims live, which are popular for holidays.

New words

Ayatollah leader of Shi'ah Muslims
Khalifah early leader of Islam
Martyr someone who dies for their faith
Paradise garden of happiness for life after death

Islam's influence

This section tells you about some of the ways in which Islam has changed the world.

Muhammad taught his friends that it was important to make the most of what Allah has given, so Muslims have always been interested in the world around them. Muslim leaders have always encouraged their people to explore areas such as science and art, and this has led to many inventions and discoveries. Hundreds of years ago, great universities and libraries were built in many Muslim cities, and became centres of learning where scholars from many countries went to study. Around 1000 CE, for example, there was a large library attached to the palace in Cairo in Egypt. Ordinary people were not only allowed to use it free of charge, they were provided with ink, pens and paper.

Medicine

Muslim doctors were the first to believe that blood circulated around the body, and they invented the first ways of treating some very serious diseases. They discovered that plants – especially herbs – could be used to treat people who were ill, and they were the first to find a way of putting patients to sleep for operations, so that it did not hurt. These discoveries were so important that their ideas were followed by other people for hundreds of years. A famous Muslim doctor was Al-Razi, who lived in Baghdad from 850 CE to 932 CE. He wrote many books, and is the first person ever known to have written about diseases in children.

Mathematics

Muslims were very interested in the science of numbers – mathematics – and the study of the stars which is called astronomy. One reason for this was because it was important to be able to work out the position of Makkah for prayer, and to be able to work out the right time for prayers. The 'Arabic system' of numbering (1, 2, 3, etc.) came first from Muslims, and early Muslims invented a calendar which is as accurate as any in use today. Algebra, trigonometry and geometry were developed by Muslim mathematicians.

Social developments

One of the sayings of Muhammad was that 'Cleanliness is half of faith', and Muslim rulers went to great lengths to make sure that their people had clean water to drink and wash in. In the tenth century CE, most towns in Europe were poor, crowded and dirty. Water came from the same stream or river where rubbish was thrown. In Muslim countries at the same time, there were houses with running water and drains, and towns were well-planned with streets, schools and public libraries. Some towns even had street-lamps which were lit at night. It was hundreds of years before people in Europe began to copy these ideas.

Muslims were the inventors of a new way of building, which meant that arches could become much slimmer and more pointed.

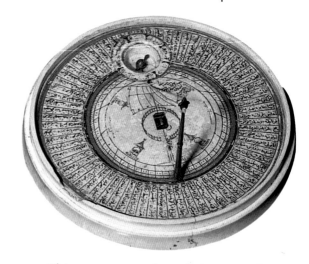

This compass and sundial was made in the sixteenth century CE

Islamic buildings are often very beautiful

This was copied by European builders, and used in many buildings which are still admired for their beauty. Muslims were also responsible for many other things which we all still use today. They brought paper to Europe, and their names for many products have become English words – 'apricot', 'sugar' and 'coffee' all started as Arabic words, and so did 'alcohol', 'jacket' and 'mattress'.

Islam's effect on the world can never be measured. Many people who have little idea about the religion use ideas and words which were first thought of by Muslims. This is a reminder that Islam is not just a religion, it is also a way of life which goes back hundreds of years.

Test yourself

What's astronomy?

Who was Al-Razi?

What are Arabic numbers?

Things to do

1 Why was providing clean water so important for early Muslim leaders?

2 Explain why Muslims have always been interested in mathematics.

3 How did trading help Islam to spread? Why do you think words like 'sugar' and 'mattress' came into English from Arabic?

4 Using information here or from other books, do a drawing and a short piece of writing explaining about something which was invented by Muslims. Why was what you have chosen important?

Islamic art

This section tells you something about art in Islam.

Why is Islamic art special?

The sort of art and decorations which Muslims use are quite special. One reason for this is that Muhammad told his friends not to draw pictures of animals or people. Only Allah can make living things, and it is wrong for human beings to try to imitate this. Muhammad was also afraid that if they made pictures or statues, they might begin to worship them. This would be idol-worship, and the Qur'an teaches that the worship of idols is totally wrong. This is because it is wrong to worship anything which is not perfect. Only Allah is perfect, therefore only Allah should be worshipped. Instead of pictures of living creatures. Muslim artists tend to concentrate on beautiful drawings of flowers and plants, and especially decorations using lines and patterns.

Some of the most beautiful examples of pattern-making are in cloths and material. The background to this is in the lives of early Muslims. In the area of the world where Islam began, many of the people were **nomads**, who spent their lives moving from place to place. Where land is almost desert, travelling is necessary to find grass for the animals. Rugs and cushions were often used instead of chairs and beds, because they are easier to carry around, and many nomads became skilled weavers of cloth. Part of their skill was making cloth attractive to look at, and many traditional patterns developed.

Anything woven by a Muslim always has a deliberate mistake. This is to avoid the weaving being perfect, because Muslims believe that only Allah can make something that is perfect. Many people who were not Muslims found the rugs and cloth attractive, too, so they became

These two photographs show how patterns are used to make beautiful decorations on buildings

important for trading. This trading is one of the ways in which Islam spread.

Calligraphy

Calligraphy is a special form of decoration. It is the name given to writing which is done so beautifully that it becomes a pattern in itself. It began when Muslims began copying the Qur'an. To write the words was considered to be a great honour, and Muslims wanted to write them as beautifully as possible. Muslim calligraphers often use quotations from the Qur'an, or from the sayings of Muhammad. The name of Allah is a favourite word for making patterns from. Writing out words and sayings like this is a way of reminding Muslims how important the words are. Many copies of the Qur'an are still hand-written today, for this reason.

Calligraphy is often used instead of pictures, because of Muhammad's teaching about not drawing living things. Patterns are used on pottery, tiles, bowls and plates as well as in embroidery and weaving. Decorations like this are often used in mosques, but they can also be seen in Muslims' homes and in other Islamic buildings. Calligraphy can also be found in the beautiful jewellery worn by Muslim women.

New words

Calligraphy the art of beautiful writing
Nomad person with no fixed home

Test yourself

What's an idol?

What's calligraphy?

What's a nomad?

Things to do

1 Explain why Muhammad forbade making pictures which included people and animals. Why do you think he felt this was so important?

2 Why do Muslims often use the name of Allah and parts of the Qur'an in their art-work?

3 Use the example of calligraphy on this page to help you write out your name or the name of someone or something important in a decorated way.

4 Find out more about Islamic art. Many libraries have specialist books about it. Choose your favourite example of a pattern, and try to copy it.

Calligraphy –
this is part of Sura 112 in the Qur'an

The Muslim family

This section tells you something about Muslim families.

The Ummah

Muslims regard all followers of Islam as being members of one big family. This is called the **Ummah**. The idea of the Ummah is very important, and helps to explain why Muslims are so concerned about other Muslims wherever they live in the world. Although it is not always the case, many Muslims feel that the fact that someone else is a follower of Islam is far more important than what country they happen to come from, or where they live.

Family life

The Qur'an says that the idea of family life comes from Allah, and playing your part in keeping your home secure and happy is seen as an important part of being a Muslim.

The Western idea of a family being just parents and children is one which Muslims do not share, and most Muslims live in **extended families** where grandparents, uncles, aunts etc. live either together or close by. Family ties are often very strong, and quite distant relatives can be thought of as 'cousins'. Children are seen as being a blessing from Allah, and so having many children is a way of showing Allah's goodness.

A Muslim family

Grandparents are important members of the family

New words

Extended family grandparents, cousins, etc. living as one family
Ummah 'community' – the wider Muslim family

Every member of a family has duties towards other members of the family. The parents' duties to their children begin with choosing a suitable name for the child. These duties continue as the child grows up, and include the responsibility of helping to choose a suitable partner for their marriage. Islam also teaches very firmly that children have duties to their parents. Elderly relatives are treated with great respect, because it is felt that their experience of life makes them wise. The Western idea of 'homes for the elderly' is one which many Muslims find quite shocking. Islam teaches that it is the duty of children to care for their parents when they are old, and Muslims believe that the place for elderly people is with the rest of the family, where they can be loved and cared for in the same way that they loved and cared for their children when they were younger. Grandparents are always seen as the head of the family.

Muslim families live together in a very open way, but family life is private. Many Muslim homes have a special guest room where male visitors can be entertained by the men. Female visitors usually stay with the women. Men and women of the family usually eat together, but when there are guests visiting women usually eat with the women of the family.

Test yourself

What's the Ummah?

What's an extended family?

Who is the head of a Muslim family?

Things to do

1 How many ways can you think of in which the idea of the Ummah might affect the daily lives of Muslims?

2 What do you think are the advantages of living in an extended family? Can you think of any disadvantages?

3 Explain why Muslims feel that grandparents and elderly people should be treated with respect.

4 Write a poem or a short story about how you might feel when you are old. How do you think the rest of the world might treat you?

Women in Islam

This section tells you something about women in Islam.

At the time of Muhammad, women were treated more or less as servants. They had very few rights, and were expected to obey men. Muhammad told Muslims that this was not what Allah wanted, and the teachings of Islam are quite different. The Qur'an says that women should be respected and cared for, and should have equal rights in education and making decisions. Under the laws of Islam, women are allowed to own things, and a woman must be present at any legal ceremony which involves her, unless she chooses to send someone else. To people brought up in Western countries, this is something that would be taken for granted, but in many Eastern countries women are very protected, and male relatives would be expected to act on their behalf.

Marriage

Muslims are expected to marry, and it is usual for the marriage to be **arranged**. This means that a woman's father or male relatives will make enquiries to see if a particular man would be suitable. (A man enquires about a woman who is recommended by his female relatives.) A suitable man would be a Muslim, because Muslim law says that children follow the religion of their father, so a non-Muslim father would mean that the children were not Muslim, either. Muslim law says that a woman cannot be forced to marry against her wishes. When she marries, a Muslim woman does not take her husband's surname. Any money or property which she owns before the marriage remains hers. So does any money which she earns if she goes out to work after the marriage. She does not have to give it to her husband unless she wants to.

Work

It is becoming more common for Muslim women to work outside the home, especially since more Muslim women than before are going on to higher education. However, many

A Muslim woman doctor

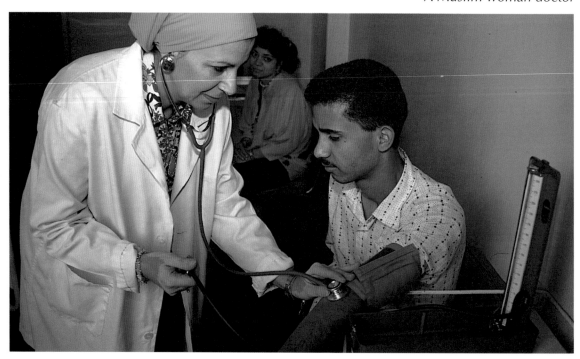

Dressing modestly and covering the head is important for Muslim women

Muslim women feel that their most important job is to create a loving home for their husband and family. The family is very important to Muslims, and husbands and wives are seen as having different – but equally important – jobs to do. It is the man's job to go out and earn money which the family needs, and it is the woman's job to look after everybody. Muslim women have the right to an extra allowance if they look after the home.

Clothes

Muslims feel that many Western women dress in ways which are not modest. They feel that wearing short, low-cut or tight clothing is intended to show off the body and 'tempt' men. This is seen as being not only unfair to men, but also degrading to women. All Muslim women should dress decently, and keep their legs and arms covered. When they are outside or with strangers, many women choose to dress so that as little as possible of their body can be seen. This includes wearing a full-length dress and a veil or scarf over their head, and is called **hijab**.

Religion

In religion, Muslim women are expected to follow the same teachings as men. However, they are not obliged to go to the mosque for the Friday prayers, so that they can be at home with their family. If she does not go to the mosque, a Muslim woman is expected to pray at home. When women worship at the mosque, they pray behind the men, or in a separate room if the prayer-hall is too small for everyone.

Test yourself

What's an arranged marriage?

What's hijab?

Things to do

1 Explain why the teaching of Islam about women was such a new idea at the time of Muhammad.

2 What do Muslims see as being a woman's most important job? Do you agree with this? Give reasons for your answer.

3 What reasons can you give why men and women in the mosque should pray separately?

4 Find some pictures in magazines of women wearing 'Western' dress. Write an article explaining why a Muslim would think that it was wrong for women to dress like this.

New words

Arranged marriage marriage where relatives make enquiries to make sure the partners are suitable
Hijab 'veil' – used to describe the modest dress worn by women

Islam in the home

This section tells you something about how Muslims live at home.

Muslims believe that their religion affects everything they do, because they have submitted their lives to Allah. The way they live at home is therefore a very important part of following their religion. This is probably especially true where they are living in a country where most people are not Muslims, because when children are not taught much about Islam at school, they will learn most of what they know from home. It is also one reason why women are thought of as being so important in Islam, because it is usually the mother who teaches the children most about the religion as they are growing up.

Most Muslim families have religious pictures on the walls. These are always placed high up as a sign of respect. Pictures which show people are never used, because the Qur'an forbids them.

Reading the Qur'an together is something that is very important for many Muslim families. The Qur'an is kept on the highest piece of furniture in the room, and nothing is ever placed on top of it. It should never be allowed to touch the floor, and is kept carefully wrapped when it is not being read.

Food

Like many other religions, Islam teaches that some foods are allowed, some are forbidden. Food which is allowed for Muslims is halal, food which is forbidden is **haram**. Anything which comes from an animal which eats other animals is haram, so is anything which comes from a pig. Fish and all fruit, grain and vegetables are halal. To be halal, an animal which is to be eaten must be killed in a special way so that all the blood is removed. Allah's name is repeated to show that the food is being taken with his permission, and the animal's throat is cut with

Muslim children learn about their religion at home

Muslims should only eat halal food

a very sharp knife, so that it becomes unconscious from loss of blood. Muslims believe that this is the kindest way of killing there is – much kinder than the usual Western methods of stunning by electric shock or a bolt fired into the skull.

If an animal is not killed so that it is halal, anything from it is haram. This includes its fat, and because animal fat can be used in a whole range of products, these may also be forbidden. This can include things such as pastry, cake and some cheeses. Food cooked in the fat of a haram animal becomes haram. Muslims who cannot buy halal products should eat only vegetarian products, because all these are allowed.

Alcohol is haram, which is why it is forbidden in Muslim countries. It is not really enough just to avoid drinking it themselves – Muslims should not be anywhere near when alcohol is being drunk. This can be a problem in Western countries, where many people's social life involves going to pubs and places which serve alcohol. Smoking is not haram, but it is discouraged because it harms the body, and Muslims believe that it is wrong to harm anything which Allah created.

New word

haram 'forbidden' – food which Muslims are not allowed to eat

Test yourself

What does 'halal' mean?

What does 'haram' mean?

Things to do

1 Why do you think that nothing is ever placed on top of a copy of the Qur'an?

2 Explain why Muslims repeat the name of Allah as an animal is killed. What does this tell you about the Muslim attitude to killing animals?

3 The Qur'an forbids Muslims to mention the name of Allah in the presence of alcohol. Why do you think this is so?

4 Working in pairs, discuss possible dishes which you could serve to a Muslim friend if he or she was coming for a meal. What would you not serve?

Muslims in Britain

This section tells you something about Muslims in Britain.

There have been Muslims living in Britain for at least two hundred years. Many of the earliest Muslims who made their homes in Britain were traders from the Middle East who settled around the major ports. After World War II, many industries in Britain were short of workers, and people came to Britain from other countries because they were promised a better life here. Many of these people were Muslims, and of course they brought their religion with them. In 1991, there were estimated to be 1.5 million Muslims in Britain.

A Muslim family in Britain

Many Muslims living in Britain were born here and have never lived in the country from which their families came. Others are British people who have chosen to **convert** to Islam. For some Muslims, life in Britain can be difficult. Their religion does not allow them to do some things which most British people do, and Western standards – for example in dress and behaviour – are very different from the standards which are expected in Muslim countries.

Religion

Islam teaches that Muslims should obey the teachings of Allah in every part of life. This means that religion has much more effect on their lives than it has on many people brought up in a Western way. For example, Muslims pray five times a day. Muslims who work outside the home or who are travelling need a clean place in which they can pray, and time to be allowed for this. Sometimes this is misunderstood by employers who are ignorant of the religion. In public places it may mean being stared at or even laughed at by people who do not understand.

Dress

Islam expects both men and women to be decently dressed. For men this means being covered from the waist to the knees, for women it means that only hands and face should be visible to men who are not relatives. From about the age of twelve, girls are expected to keep their arms, legs and head covered. Sometimes this can cause problems at school, especially in lessons such as PE and swimming.

Relationships

Muslim children are not expected to mix with the opposite sex once they become teenagers. This, too, can be a problem in school. Girls are

Young Muslim girls keep their legs covered for PE

not expected to go out alone with boys. When they wish to marry, their parents will help them to choose a partner because they care about them and have had more experience of life. Many young Muslims prefer to leave such an important decision to older relatives. They feel that the idea of going out with someone before marriage is like being in a market where people pick and choose the best product. Some young Muslims do not feel like this, however. They see friends choosing partners, and feel that they should be able to do the same. This can cause enormous heartache for them and their families.

Medical treatment

Muslims do not think that it is right for a woman to be examined by a male doctor, or a man by a woman doctor. If this is not understood, it can cause problems in hospital, where there is usually no choice about which doctor you see.

New word

Convert to become a member of a religion

Test yourself

Roughly how many Muslims are there in Britain?

From what age are girls expected to keep their body covered?

Things to do

1 Working in groups, how many difficulties can you think of which British Muslims might have in following their religion? How many ways can you think of in which non-Muslims could make things easier for Muslims?

2 How many reasons can you think of why Muslims believe that girls and boys should not be allowed to mix?

3 Why might an 'arranged' marriage be a good idea? What reasons are there why it might be a bad idea?

4 If possible, talk to a Muslim living in Britain about their life and their religion.

Special occasions I

This section tells you about the special things which happen to Muslim children.

Birth

Muslims believe that life is a gift from Allah. As soon as a baby is born, he or she is washed, and the adhan (Call to prayer) is whispered into the right ear. Then the 'Command to worship' is whispered into the left ear. This means that the first words a baby hears are the most important words of the Muslim faith. Then a tiny piece of sugar or honey is placed on the baby's tongue. This is a custom which comes from the Hadith, and may be done by the parents or the child's oldest relative. Some people think it is a symbol of making the child 'sweet' – kind and obedient.

Aqiqah

The **aqiqah** ceremony takes place when the baby is seven days old. According to the Hadith, a goat or a sheep should be sacrificed to give thanks to Allah for the arrival of the baby. At least a third of the meat is given to the poor. Today, animals may not always be sacrificed. Instead, a donation of money is given to the poor.

The baby is given its name at the ceremony. Choosing a name for the baby is one of the important duties of parents. Sometimes the name chosen is a family name, sometimes it is one of Muhammad's names, or one of his family. All Muslim names have a meaning. A common choice for boys is one of the 99 names of Allah, with 'Abd' in front of it. Abd means 'servant' in Arabic, so this is a way of saying that the child will be a servant of Allah. It is quite common for parents to stop using their own names when their first child is born, and become known as 'father of' and 'mother of'. For example, if the child was called Muhammad, the father would be known as 'Abu Muhammad' and the mother as 'Umm Muhammad'.

At the aqiqah, the baby's head is shaved, and olive oil is sometimes rubbed in as a symbol of cleanliness. The hair which has been cut off is weighed, and the value of an equal weight in silver is given to the poor. Male babies are **circumcised** soon after birth. This means that the foreskin is removed from the end of the penis. It is quite a common operation.

Whispering the adhan to a new baby

At the madrasah

Attending the madrasah

From about the age of four, a child is expected to go to the **madrasah** regularly. This is the special school held at the mosque, where children learn to read and write Arabic, and recite the Qur'an. They are also taught the correct way to pray, and how to perform wudu, the special washing before prayers.

New words

Aqiqah naming ceremony
Circumcision removal of the foreskin from the penis
Madrasah school at the mosque

Test yourself

Why is honey put on the baby's tongue?

What's the aqiqah?

What's the madrasah?

Things to do

1 What do you think it means to be a 'servant of Allah'?

2 Why do you think Muslims place such importance on a child's name? Do you think your name makes any difference to the person you are?

3 Explain how giving to the poor is part of the celebration of a baby's birth. Why do you think this is so?

4 Explain what Muslim boys and girls are expected to learn at the madrasah.

Special occasions II

This section tells you about special events which happen in a Muslim's life.

Marriage

Muslims are encouraged to marry, and few stay single all their life. Sexual relationships outside of marriage are disapproved of very strongly. Muslim marriages are usually 'arranged' (see page 38). Both partners have to agree before the marriage can take place. The marriage ceremony is not a religious one. All the details of the marriage are set out in a contract, which is a legal document. It can contain almost anything which the couple wish to make a

An Indian Muslim bride and bridegroom

condition of the marriage. (It could not include anything which would go against the purpose of marriage – for example, a condition not to live together.) The groom gives the bride a gift of money, which remains hers even if he later divorces her.

The Qur'an says that a man can have up to four wives, but only if he can treat them all exactly the same. Today, this is usually seen as meaning that a man should only marry once, because it is obviously impossible to treat different people in exactly the same way. Some men do take a second wife, if the first cannot have children, or becomes ill and needs someone to look after her. This can only happen if the first wife agrees. (It cannot happen in Britain, where marrying more than one person at a time is against the law.)

Divorce

Divorce is strongly discouraged in Islam, and it is often seen as a disgrace to the families if a marriage breaks down. Friends and relatives try hard to help a couple who are having difficulties. If divorce cannot be avoided, Muslim law says that the wife has the right to take all her belongings from the house. Once the divorce is final, her former husband has no further responsibility for her. She is usually looked after by her male relatives, because Muslim women are not encouraged to work. Muslims who have been divorced may marry again if they wish.

Death

If he or she can speak, the last words a dying Muslim will say are the Shahadah – 'There is only one God and Muhammad is his prophet'. After death, the body is washed (preferably by relatives) and wrapped in white sheets, often the ihram sheets from Hajj. Muslims are always

A Muslim funeral in Spain

buried, never **cremated**. They believe that the body will be re-created and resurrected at the Day of Judgement. Funerals should be simple, and Muslims prefer that the body should be in contact with the earth, rather than in a coffin. After prayers, the body is buried with the head and right side facing Makkah. If possible, Muslims prefer to bury a body on the day of death.

After death

Muslims believe in **akhirah** – everlasting life after death. They believe that this life is a test, and angels will tell Allah about the way each person has behaved on earth. Allah will then judge what each person has deserved. Those who have earned it will go to Paradise, a beautiful garden of peace, joy and contentment. Those who disobeyed and rejected Allah in their life on earth will go to **Hell** where they will suffer for ever.

New words

Akhirah everlasting life after death
Cremation burning a body after death
Hell place of punishment for life after death

Test yourself

What's cremation?

What's Paradise?

What's Hell?

Things to do

1 What do you think of the idea of a marriage contract? What sort of things might it include?

2 Explain the Muslim attitude to divorce.

3 Why do you think that where possible Muslims bury a body in the ihram sheets which the person used on Hajj?

4 Many religions teach that we will be judged after death by the way we have lived on earth. What do you think about this? Discuss your ideas in small groups, then write up your discussion.

5 Write a poem or draw a picture to show what you would like Paradise to be like.

Glossary

Adhan call to prayer
Akhirah everlasting life after death
Allah Arabic name for God, used by all Muslims
Angel Jibril messenger of Allah
Aqiqah naming ceremony
Arabic language used in Muslim worship, and spoken by some Muslims
Arranged marriage marriage where relatives make enquiries to make sure the partners are suitable
Ayatollah leader of Shi'ah Muslims

Calligraphy the art of beautiful writing
Christianity religion of Christians
Circumcision removal of the foreskin from the penis
Convert to become a member of a religion
Cremation burning a body after death

Day of Judgement end of the world, when Allah will judge everyone
Devil spirit of evil
Dome roof shaped like half a ball
Du'a personal prayers

Eternal lasting for ever
Extended family grandparents, cousins, etc. living as one family

Fasting doing without food and drink for religious reasons

Hadith teachings based on the life of Muhammad
Hafiz person who has learned the Qur'an by heart
Hajj pilgrimage to Makkah
Halal 'allowed' – food which Muslims can eat
Haram 'forbidden' – food which Muslims are not allowed to eat
Hell place of punishment for life after death
Hijab 'veil' – used to describe the modest dress worn by women
Hijrah 'departure' – name given to Muhammad's journey to Madinah

Idol statue worshipped as a god
Ihram special way of living for Hajj (also the special clothes)
Imam Muslim leader and teacher

Jihad struggle against evil
Judaism religion of Jews

Ka'bah most important place of Muslim worship
Khalifah early leader of Islam

Madrasah school at the mosque
Martyr someone who dies for their faith
Meditate to think deeply, especially about religion
Mihrab arch in the wall which shows the direction of Makkah
Minaret tower of a mosque
Minbar platform used for preaching
Mosque Muslim place of worship
Mu'adhin man who calls Muslims to prayer
Muslim follower of the religion of Islam

Nomad person with no fixed home

Paradise garden of happiness for life after death
Pilgrimage journey for religious reasons
Prophet someone who tells people what Allah wants

Qur'an Muslim holy book

Rak'ah set of positions for Muslim prayers
Recitation repeating something learned by heart
Retreat special time of praying and thinking

Sacrifice offering made to a God
Scriptures holy books
Sins 'wrong-doing' – something which separates a person from God
Submission 'yield' – obey someone else's authority
Surah chapter in the Qur'an
Symbol something that stands for something else

Ummah 'community' – the wider Muslim family
Umrah 'lesser pilgrimage'

Vision dream-like religious experience

Wudu special washing before prayer
Wuquf 'stand before Allah' – most important part of Hajj